CRYSTAL WRIGHT

December
MOODS

Inquiries and Book Orders should be addressed to:

Great Writers Media
Email: info@greatwritersmedia.com
Phone: (302) 918-5570

ISBN: 978-1-961416-55-0 (sc)
ISBN: 978-1-961416-56-7 (ebk)

Rev 02/02/2022

Red river

River cry
River cry
It was the red river crimson tide,
That ran through me
They were running when he parted the Red Sea.
Boats surged
And I felt the urge
To sound the shofar
So they could hear it from afar.
River cry
River cry
I saw the river rise
Just as the sun was set to rise
Eluding the daggers and arrows bow.
The bow signaled his promise to earth.
Hurry! hurry! he is heading this way.
Scuffling with the keys to open the gate way.
Moving onward
It was a time of exodus.
The river turned red, from all of the blood shed.
River cry
River cry
The river cries tears of blood.
The hour glass has flipped
Bringing forth something new
It doesn't know why, so it continues to cry.
It was something that was devised.

—CJW

Gemstone

Paul came to town
What he had on his mind was this lovely gem stone
He heard stories of it while growing up.
he set out to find this gemstone.
Paul traveled far and wide to find it.
He traveled the whole world.
He was left with one last place to look.
Paul reached this island, and searched it for this gem
He couldn't find it so he began to give up.
Just as he was going to give up
He met this girl.
She'd been watching him, wondering what the hell he was looking for.
She went over to talk to him and he told her what he was looking for.
People always asked him what he looked for, and when he told
them Not many believed.
But, he told her and she believed.
She told him she would help him find this gem.
So they did look for it together.
They still can't find it.
They decide to take a break from looking. They ended up spending
the night out together laughing and talking.
They wandered off to a cave.
They saw a lot of beautiful things.
They end up staying up until the morning.
They knew it was morning because there was a crack in the caves
ceiling and it offered light.
Where this light shine they stood.
As they stood she felt something beneath her feet.
They looked down and there it was, the gemstone.

Amazed at their finding they hugged each other.

But something wasn't quite right.

Paul had a change of heart. He's found what he had been looking for. Paul wanted the gem for himself but he changed. All what he's been looking for he finally found but it felt empty.

He knew what he had to do.

Paul took this gemstone and stretched out his arm towards her. He said "give me your hand"

She was hesitant, but she gave him her hand.

He smiled and said, "I don't even know your name" She smiled back and said "Ruby, My name is Ruby"

He placed the gem in her hand and told her she could have it.

What he's spent his whole life looking for and told himself he would keep, he gave it all away to her.

But he realized that he found something more than what he bargained for. He found a wonderful friend, who is also a gem, and she was a lovely Ruby.

He couldn't ask for anything more.

His life had been changed and it had just begun.

He did not find just one, but two gemstones.

—CJW

Truth is...

Sometimes we are not always happy.
Sometimes we are not always sad.
Sometimes you'll find peace.
Sometimes that peace will be dismantled, then you have to find it all over again.
Sometimes you'll be disappointed.
Sometimes you will be rewarded.
Sometimes you know, while sometimes you don't
Sometimes we spend our whole life looking for something that will not be found.
Sometimes we find things, that we weren't even looking for.
Sometimes there are days when you don't even want to live.
Sometimes there are days where you want nothing more than to live.
Sometimes you don't know what you want, while on other days you do know.
Sometimes we all cry at some point in our lives.
Sometimes we don't get it right even when we try.
Sometimes people don't accept you, because they are stuck in their ways.
Sometimes people help, sometimes they don't.
Sometimes God answers, sometimes he doesn't.
Sometimes society creates monsters out of men.
Sometimes not everyone has their shit together, sometimes they don't even know how to get their shit together.
So truth is, these are the things that really happens instead of falsified beliefs and pretending.
Truth is we pretend more than just being because just being for some is much harder than pretending.

—CJW

2:30am

Ring, Ring...
"Hello"
I hear a hesitant voice
"Hello" I say again.
Then i hear your voice say,
"Hi"
I say "Hi, how are you, are you okay?"
You say "I'm fine, yes I'm okay. I just wanted to hear your
    voice,"
I smile and say, "well can you hear it?"
You laugh out, with a reply, "yes, very clear"
We fall into a silence.
I can hear you breathing.
"Ca...,"
"What is it?"
"You take a deep breath, and say "can you come over?"
"Sure, give a couple mins, I'll be on my way"

....

Tap, tap!
Two knocks on your door.
I hear the door unlock, and see the door open slowly.
I see you standing there smiling
I smile as well.
"Come in"
In I step and follow your lead.
We've found our selves on your couch.

Chatting for a while, until I hear a song come on, on the music that
was being played.
I stood up and reached out my hand, signaling you to take my hand.
You shook your head saying no.
"Come on, don't be such a platter puss," I whined.
You finally took my hand, and we danced in each other's arms.
The music ends, along with our dance.
We embraced in a hug, then pulled apart just enough to look in
each other's eyes.
Wow, you are one of the most beautiful things I've come to love.

—CJW

Black hole

Let me sink into you like a space probe lost in the darkness of the
black hole.
Take me away.
Let me get lost in your depths like a black hole.
I am black but I am not whole.
With you I will be whole.
I fell into your hole where there was light within me and we became
one with the black hole.
I am mysterious as a black hole
You are as large as a black hole.
No one really knows of us, just like a black hole.
So be my black hole and I'll be your Milky Way.
What would become of us when we collide?
Will you become light like the Milky Way?
Or will I become black as you?
We come close and do a dance.
We twirl and swirl and blend our moods
Which creates wonders and a wonderful sighting for scientists.
I won't ever let you go.
When you are light years away from me and I stand on the floor
and look up at you?
I will never forget the love that we shared.
I will remember you in the next lifetime.
You are my black hole.
Maybe one day you will swallow up everything whole and I will
become one with you.
You are my black hole, don't you get it.

I love your space
I love you whole
You are my black hole.
You are the black hole.

—CJW

Hopeless Romantic

Two lovers who are hopeless romantics.
Romantic whenever, hopeless together.
They hold out their hearts for each other.
They try not to hurt each other.
Even though they are hopeless, they find hope within each other,
    that's what makes it romantic.
All aboard, let's take a trip all around the world on the new titanic.
Since when does the sea have so much traffic?
We are being followed for our platonic love.
"Should we go under cover?" he asks.
"We should, let's go under seas" she replies. "I'll have a subma-
    rine waiting at the port. We won't be plagued under the sea."
    "Should we take refuge under sea
We should, let's make our love like Ariel and Eric" It doesn't matter
    if we are worlds apart
Or worldly different I'll love you like no other.
I was blessed with unconditional love.
I've never loved like this.
I'll find you wherever
Whether this life time or the next.
I won't forget you, even if you do.
My soul has been found, since we met.
I love you
I love you
My dearest love.
You are my hopelessness
You are my romantic

Without you I will be frantic.
It is you, who makes me a hopeless romantic.
I don't care, I love it.

—CJW

Eye witness

My eyes is my camera and my brain is my memory card for that camera.

My eyes witnessed a hard working woman who's sweat turned into tears.

My eyes witnessed the softness of her heart, turning into a rock hard heart, but still being able to give love.

My eyes witnessed the lonely and hurtful times being drowned away with music.

My eyes witnessed her wanting to be loved.

My eyes witnessed the true love she has for her children.

My eyes witnessed the sacrifices made for her children to live.

My eyes witnessed the happy to the sad times.

My eyes witnessed the pleads for the heavens to hear her prayers.

My eyes witnessed her wanting that change for years.

My eyes witnessed her devotion and persistence to keep on moving.

My eyes witnessed her powerful authority like voice.

My eyes witnessed her mighty and wonderful laugh.

My eyes witnessed her sense of humor.

Yes, my eyes witnessed her,

She is a beautiful angel sent by God trying to find her way.

Her eyes and my eyes connect, her eyes are brown.

In those eyes they witnessed me witnessing her.

She has long flowing locs hanging down the side of her face. It is black from the root down and at the end, it has a burn orange color.

She has the most beautiful smile.

Her lips and teeth looks like it had been carved beautifully, there are no mistakes.

She is perfect from head to toe.

My eyes witnessed the beauty that she doesn't see.

My eyes witnessed and cherishes the sighting of an angel.

I ask her her name, and she says "my name is Barbara Angella Morrison." She is my mother, my father, and my friend.

She is everything I don't have, she fills me up.

I am happy for my camera and for all the beautiful pictures and wonderful moments it captured.

It is called my eyes, and these eyes gave me the chance to see and witness.

—CJW

Scar

A four inch knife is embedded in my heart.
Every time my heart beats, it penetrates a vein, heals itself, and
    leaves a scar.
My blood cells bleeds water.
I am tainted with hurt, diluting my being with pain, along with a
    little mixture of happiness.
I drive to the woods, wearing all white to coverup my dark state of
    mind.
Nothin but bushes, trees and animals.
I cry out from the root of my implanted bare feet on the ground, to
    the hair follicles on my head.
I take off all of my clothes and spread them on the ground.
The naked eye of nature could see my destruction.
A part of me liked the pain, so I began to run.
Speeding up my hearts beat so that I could be stabbed repeatedly,
    over and over again.
The other part of me wanted to get away from the pain; so I took a
    stone and killed two emotions.
I made up my mind to run.
To run until I reach a faulty destination.
I ran and ran, on and on.
There was no turning back now.
I ran into a trance.
I could see the inner paleness of my left palm.
I see a two inch scar on my left pinky finger, this scar was from my
    month old ages.
I was a child when this scar became.
This young scar grew into my old body.
I could see a trail in my palm forming.

When I looked closely, I could see that it was me.
I could see myself on the heart line of my palm.
I was a palm reader when it was too late.
I fall out of trance.
In the distance I could see a gap but I kept on running.
Closer and closer I reach, I take a last look behind.
Only my eyes could turn back now.
Down I go, any longer running; my view of behind started to fade.
I am falling off this cliff.
My back is towards the down and my eyes towered to the sky.
What a beautiful sighting?
I was relaxed.
I didn't fight the fall, I just eloped into it.
"Splash"
I am a wrecking ball to this brick of water.
Crashing through and kept on going.
I can't hold my breath no longer, I take in a limitless amount of
      water; my inner and outer being is engulfed with water.
I am sunken to unknown treasures.
A fools gold.
I am gold to a fool, which fool will find me now?
A wound became a scar and a scar takes form.
I am no longer around to trace over these untraceable scars, the
      water will freeze me up to preserve all of these vicious scars.
Fluctuating my broken fall and embracing my indigenous faults.

—CJW

It's funny/ I wonder/ whatever happened

It's funny how, people make love seems like it's an animal, when really they're the ones who is really the animal.

I wonder, when will be the day God comes, and will I be living?

Whatever happened to true love, romance, loyalty and respect?

It's funny how, everyone and everything has its purpose on this earth and people just can't seem to see that.

I wonder, what happened to the first bible ever written?

Whatever happened to loving and caring?

It's funny how, people can't seem to see and believe that there is a God; when you see and hear about back to back earthquakes, tornadoes and volcanic eruptions.

I wonder, will I make it to heaven?

Whatever happened to the testimonies, prophets and the disciples?

It's funny how our body works.

I wonder, what will happen to all of humanity?

Whatever happened to the human race, and what have we become?

It's funny how a stranger could treat me better than my family. I wonder, when will it be my time?

Whatever happened to preaching the truth about the word? It's funny how I wonder about whatever happened.

—CJW

Unique flower

I am a flower deep in the forest, nowhere to be found by the humans.
I am apart of the daisy family because I always daze off into thoughts.
The wind blows and pushes me from side to side, I am being bullied in love.
The wind feels mellow and weird at the same time over my leaves.
I take a shower when the lovely rain falls.
I dry when the sun shines its rays upon my petals.
My home is nature.
I have always been a loner, since my growing day.
A bee comes around and buzzed and whisks pass my ear.
He goes to my fellow flower and lands on it.
It caresses that flower, it takes its life away and then flies away.
I question myself, why doesn't the bee ever land on me?
But I now know that I am different; the bee always went to the flowers that were weak.
He never came to me because I had a water mark, that made me standout from the rest, and it made me strong.
Thank you to the one or two human that came to the forest because they noticed me; when they read this or heard this.
They left me the way they saw me, but they gave me more strength and power the moment they saw me.
I was hidden where no human could find me.
They were sent to give me hope and courage, to keep on growing.

—CJW

Butterfly

Butterfly in subways
It rides the train with the on goers
Its white complexion meshes with the rainbow colors of the riders
It flies ever so delicately
With grace and passion
Why do the fragile, ride with iron giants?
I guess it's here, to give us a sense of calmness from heavy plated
world
I forgot how lost I was in thoughts, until you appeared.
I almost forgot myself.
I couldn't dream with you.
You should have brought more of your friends.
Shucks, I have to go.
I made my transfer, leaving you behind.
I wonder, will you remember me?
Would you visit me again tomorrow?
May I see you again?
Will you miss me as much as I miss you?
Can you entertain me again, with one last ride?
Can you come visit me in my repeated dreams?
Keep me company in the stormy misadventures.
Be my friend until the very end.
Butterfly
Butterfly
Won't you just teach me how to fly?

—CJW

Decoded

How do you decode decoded?

just find decode and it'll be decoded.

If you can't get this to decode it, just put a coat over it and it'll be coated.

It'll keep you safe from the cold, sike.

Man, you know the cold isn't sugar coated.

If that was the case, I'd be feeling warm walking around in this coat in the twenties.

Decoding the Bible, the Bible is really the word of God, that the devil used to put the veil over our eyes, evil decoded

Take off the D off of decoded and add it to evil, and you'll see the devil decoded.

The devil lived, so he taught us his way to live and we followed him and got caught on his catch, now that's his kill.

No mother fucker really, that's his skill.

Now because of this, a lot of us have strayed from our own will.

Now we are trying to find the code to get back to the safe, I mean the safe side of dying.

Well, at least only some.

The ones that choose to be the chosen ones.

I hope you can read this Morse code and get the message I sent, and not be like the ones that received it but returned it to sender.

How splendor!

That was sarcasm If you didn't notice.

Oh wait, you were probably in the race running with the ism and made it to the finish line, in this racism

Or you were just too busy, being a judge in this court house called system.

Now, they are living life in a blender, putting hell on earth, but together they'll be drinking of that mighty health shake.

If you paid attention, then you'd probably notice this 7.7 magnitude earth quake, or do you want me to take it back to Harlem and hit em with the shake.

Man, it's time for us to awake.

So find the code and go on the road to return to the one.

Be that one, to find the one, to make you become the chosen one. Then you can put back the code in decoded and leave it for someone else to find the code and simply decode it.

—CJW

Dream sessions

Dreaming dreams in dreams, Martin Luther king tells us that he has a dream.

Michael reflected his dream with a man in the mirror.

Malcolm X marks the spot in this dream of hidden treasures.

John Lennon, dreamed of having peace in all of the ages.

Tupac was a thug in his life of dreams, for the youths.

Bob Marley saw the dream of a natural mystic combined with his one love.

Jimmi Hendrix played the dream all over his guitar strings.

Lauryn Hill dreamed of freeing all of her sons.

Marvin Gaye song the love that he loved within a dream.

Elvis Presley chose to be comfortable rocked out in jumpers in his dream.

Whitney Houston will always love you in her caring dream.

While many come up and dream, dreams of bringing forth a dream; they will not recognize that Biggie was right when he said "it was all a dream."

You're sleep walking while you're dreaming, so you speed up to try and chase that living dream.

The thing about dreams are, you're always dreaming.

I love the day, because I dream a wonderful day dream and I love the night, because it brings out the mere effect on elm street.

This dream can be cut short, due to interruptions from death, the dream catcher or you can simply awake from a dream, that leads you back to a dream with Alzheimer's.

I had a dream, but what was it about?

I can't remember.

The only thing I know is, that it was all a dream.

Oh well, I'll just keep living out this dream with my eyes wide open
and dream of having dreams.
While, dreaming of those dreams; I will dream a dreaming dream.
I was developed from a living dream, that has plenty more dreams.
So it all comes down to the part where I'm living in dream sessions.
This dream will never end.

—CJW

Last breath

That was the last time, I took a deep breath, laughed and cried at
 once.
I held my breath from death, it couldn't take my last breath.
That last breath was not for death.
I saved it for someone else.
I wave an arm; suggesting, come hither mother.
She proceeds unto my deal.
I opened her mouth and gave her my last breath.
I've given her added years.
One of three who gave me life.
She played her role, along with the other two.
She was there
She bred me
And I could see her.
Her love made me promise to be obligated to her, without her even
 saying it.

—CJW

Water bed

I am a princess to this queen size wooden bed, sleeping without a king size pillow trying to get away from my high ranking duties.

Laying in plushies and worries, I begin to feel myself sinking into the mattress.

Drowning me in sorrow and misery.

It feels like the boogie man has been keeping an eye on me.

I was dreaming that I wet the bed, just to wake up and find myself in a wet bed.

I'm not even going to move.

Crickets chirp outside my window, crying to the darkness while the moon stands and stare.

I am in this bed, and I can travel to anywhere; but it doesn't matter, not this time.

Sleep takes me to places that I belong, but when I'm awake I don't belong.

I'm in the wrong place at the right time, but I'm just trying to make it back home in time.

I saw what I could see and saw not what I couldn't, now I'm just ready for something new.

—CJW

Colors of war

Blacks and caucasians; the two major skin tones that is wrapped in a rainbow to conceive many races of people.

What they have in common, is the war they face unwillingly and the war they fight knowingly.

John never wanted to go to war, because he feared that he would die.

He got drafted and went to war and lived.

He came back home thinking it was safe, but war came to him, and he died where he thought he lived.

The art of war is raw.

Creating odors that is foul to the order of humanity.

How will we grow, if we take the life of each other?

There will be no one to grow.

We can take the colors that we are, to create a war that is consist of love.

Create a canvas that can show that we are kind and happy.

Execute all selfishness and unbalance ways.

Create an evolution, where we can all evolve.

Evolve tells us to love, my good friends.

Who's ready to evolve with love and forget about the war that causes us to destroy?

—CJW

Grandfather clock

A dark brown and grey headed grandfather clock stands in my life.
His height shadowed over my siblings and I.
He worked just fine.
Keeping us on time with respect and care.
His pendulum heart beats back and forth with chimes.
He played a lovely sound when he preached.
He couldn't read, but he knew the Bible like he lived in it.
Although he couldn't read, we would read his time with handed
    down seconds.
His carving genes could not be lost, because it was imprinted on
    his grandchildren.
People knew the time when they saw us
This clock was all I saw in my numbered ages, until it struck 6 pm.
As time grew with me, my heart started to beat in slow motion,
    barely holding itself together, it was only dust.
I migrated to another place, leaving my grandfather clock at its
    ticking destination.
I missed my grandfather clock every hour and second hand that
    made up days.
He struck twelve and never moved again.
Eighty seven, sixty minutes passed for a completed rotation in his
    living ticks.
He predicted the exact time for his pendulum to stop swinging.
He stopped working on the thirteenth day, in the tenth month, in
    the two thousand and eleven decade period.
His pendulum had a crack in it, called a heart attack.
My grandfather clock died from a heart break.
I wasn't even around to dust and polish him off.

I went for a trip to his destination two years earlier, but he had a touch of Alzheimer's.

I'm not sure if he knew who I was.

This broke my mind, and to hear later that he passed on was paralyzingly hurtful.

I almost couldn't make it to his framed gathering of being laid to rest.

He was preserved as best as possible for a month.

He was buried on the twelve day, in the eleventh month, in the two thousand and eleven decade period.

At 1pm on our watches.

My grandfather clock was no more.

No more ticks or sound, he stood quiet.

My grandfather clock is one of the greatest antiques that I will ever own in life.

He was known to me as "grandfather" (William Clinton Wright) and I miss him dearly.

—CJW

Fly away

I beg of you, let me fly away.

Let me fly away, like doves released out of many cages.

Let me fly away, like a balloon that got away from its string and floats upwards toward the sun.

Let me fly away, like a passenger jet in the sky without a landing gear.

Let me fly away, like smoke to the sky.

Let me fly away, like an eye view to the stars. Let me fly away, like a newborn bird learning to fly. Let me fly away, like a rocket to mars.

Let me fly away, like a satellite to a spy.

Let me fly away, like a mind without wings.

Fly me far away, so that I may be lost but will not lose.

Let me be the wings of a flyer, flying away.

Fly me away with freeness and love.

I need to get away.

Help me, to fly away.

Please, I want to fly away.

—CJW

Painter

How can you call yourself a painter, if you do not paint? Oh, but I am a painter.

I am a painter of emotions.

I paint with tears, which brings forth an art filled with happiness and sadness.

The two main back bones of emotions.

A painter does not need to have a paint brush nor paint to be a painter.

Painters comes in all forms.

A sky is a painter of clouds and stars, just to name a few.

A book is a painter of sheets and words, just to name another few.

We are the painted, in the Frame of a painters vision.

We are the painted to the earth.

The earth is the painted to the sky and universe, and the universe is the painted to the unknown.

Even the living and the dead paints.

One of my favorite masterpiece of art is, the tie dye tumble washing of many colors in the sky.

It never ceases to amaze me.

Mazes paint the confusion to a mind to stay trapped, or escape by a thin line of blockage.

The flesh on a bone, grabs hold for dear life, until it loses grip and falls to its death, by the painters expiration.

The painters and paintings are all around, if we see them for who they are and they are all that we see, everywhere we go.

Anywhere we choose to reside and anywhere we choose to hide, they are painting us, while we are painting them.

That is a painters best treasures and it is filled with colors from the painted divine.

—CJW

A thirsty will

Limes turning into lemons
They whither away to produce flowing juices to quench a poor
mans thirst.
His thirst is quenched but his hunger remains.
He hungers for words from his untied tongue to flee to the ears of
a deaf mans cry.
A deaf man cries to be heard, but what does he hear for him to cry
in such a hurtful way?
He doesn't have to hear a thing to feel the hurt that runs audibly
through his mind.
I look unto him and say " I could hear you sir, so please don't cry"
He turns to me and says, " I cry for you my love, for you are not
deaf but no one hears you."
"Oh but only one hears me," I say. "Only you, dear good sir, only
you" In sign language.
He smiles and says "I know who to listen to, I may be deaf but
when someone is sent for me to listen, I hear them very well."
Everyone hears, but we choose to disobey the person with the
words, who sadly doesn't fit the criteria for our ears to listen.
A lion is a king of the jungle, but what happens to his thrown when
the jungle decides to disappear?
He's meek to the earth behind that mighty roar, so why do we
choose to capture him when he's really weak?
What good is the light, when all you see is darkness?
Will you wait for the lime to grow old to become a lemon or will
you eat the lime while it's young?
What really is the decision here, when they both make you cringe
from its taste?
Is that the only choices you have between the two antidotes?

—CJW

Humanoid

Standing in the middle of the world, I struggle to breathe.

I need my inhaler; a dose of breath captured in a portable container. I search my sandy gray pockets, the left pocket is barely attached and

the right pocket is stable enough to hold the antidote to my survival.

My black T-shirt had a feast with holes, but I didn't care.

I wore what I had and I liked the fact that the holes were there with me. The holes are art, they wanted to be seen, so they came around and I let them stay.

They enjoyed my company and I did theres.

I didn't make them feel like an outlaw, like how society set them up to be in the fashion world.

I made them in laws instead.

My family loves them.

I looked around in my standing position, the people around me moved like robots.

The earth itself was suffocating.

The sky lost its colors, it was replaced with only one.

There were grey clouds everywhere, but yet it never rained.

The ground was crying out through the dried cracks in its sound. The sky and the ground cried incomplete, they both had the sound with no tears, it was such a drought.

My big toe touched the ground through the hole in my right footed sneaker.

I called it the sneak-flops.

It was a sneaker at the top and a flip flop at the bottom.

The rubber on the bottom was ripping off.

When I walked, you would hear the sound of which a flip flop made.

Although it never rained, the ocean remained.

There was no more waves or sound, the ocean stood still.
Something beautiful is dying.
I copied the spaces in my mind to try to fill the void, it failed.
It only pasted emptiness.
There are piles of dust, which were actually bodies lying on the ground with dead critters and plants.
They all decayed.
The wind blew and swept them all out of the way.
Gone with the wind.
Now every time the wind blew I felt the touch of someone touching me.
A stranger, I suppose.
Another attack, I reached into my pocket to find my last breath.
I put it to my mouth and squeezed away.
There was only eight seconds to live.
Four seconds for future living and four seconds of flashbacks.
My inhaler was finished and so was I.
My last flash happens and I see of the love that started but is now dying. Just like the others, I will be carried off into the wind to transparent living with a lot of loving feeling

—CJW

www.ingramcontent.com/pod-product-compliance
Lightning Source LLC
Chambersburg PA
CBHW070955120626
46546CB00004B/1628